501 PHRASES GREAT TEACHERS SAY OFTEN

DR DHEERAJ MEHROTRA

Contents

Preface

Teaching is a profession of inspiration, guidance, and connection. Words can shape students' confidence, ignite their curiosity, and build their resilience. Great teachers understand the profound impact of their words, using them not just to educate but to empower and uplift.

501 Phrases Great Teachers Say Often celebrates the language of encouragement, wisdom, and empathy that defines exceptional educators. This book captures the expressions and phrases that motivate students, foster trust, and cultivate a positive learning environment.

From affirmations of effort like "You've got this!" to reflective prompts such as "What do you think about this idea?" these phrases serve as practical tools for every teacher's daily interactions. They emphasize the importance of recognizing individual potential, promoting collaboration, and nurturing a growth mindset in students.

This collection isn't just about words; it's about the values they represent—respect, curiosity, patience, and a deep belief in the power of education. Whether you're a seasoned educator or just beginning your journey, these phrases will enrich your communication and help you leave a lasting impact on your students' lives.

Let this book inspire and remind you of the profound influence every teacher carries through their words. Together, let's create classrooms where students not only learn but thrive.

www.authordheerajmehrotra.com

1
Great Teachers Say

Encouragement and Positivity

"You've got this!"

- *"Keep trying; you're almost there!"*

- *"Your effort makes me proud "*

- *"Every day, you're getting better "*

- *"Mistakes are proof you're learning "*

- *"You're doing amazing work!"*

- *"I love your enthusiasm "*

- *"That's a brilliant idea "*

- *"Your growth is inspiring "*

- *"Don't be afraid to ask questions "*

Motivating to Overcome Challenges

"Problems are opportunities to learn "

"You can solve this if you keep at it "

"Let's break this into smaller steps "

"Think about how far you've come!"

"You're braver than you think "

"The harder you work, the luckier you get "

"I believe in your abilities "

"Failure is just the beginning of success "

"What can we learn from this experience?"

"Don't give up now—you're so close "

Building Confidence

"Your opinion matters "

"You're unique and special "

"You've made a great observation "

"I trust your judgment "

"You've got a natural talent for this "

"You're an important part of this team "

"That's an excellent question "

"Your creativity shines in this work "

"You can teach others what you've learned "

"You should feel proud of yourself "

Promoting Kindness and Teamwork

"Be the reason someone smiles today "

"How can we support each other better?"

"Listening is as important as speaking "

"Let's celebrate everyone's success "

"Helping others makes us stronger "

"You did a great job working together "

"Respect goes both ways "

"Kindness always counts "

"Let's lift each other up "

"Teamwork makes the dream work "

Engagement in Learning

"Who can connect this to what we learned yesterday?"

- "What do you think will happen next?"

- "Can you explain it in your own words?"

- "Why do you think this is important?"

- "Let's think critically about this "

- "What other ways could we solve this?"

- "Let's explore this further "

- "I'd love to hear your perspective "

- "Who has a different approach to share?"

- "Your questions guide our learning "

-

-

-

Praising Effort

"I see how hard you're working "

"Effort always pays off "

"You're improving every day "

"Hard work builds strong habits "

"It's okay to struggle; it's part of growing "

"You're pushing your limits, and it's impressive "

"Practice makes progress "

"Your dedication is inspiring "

"Small steps lead to big achievements "

"You've come so far already "

Reflective Thinking

"What would you do differently next time?"

- "How did you reach that conclusion?"

- "What have you learned from this process?"

- "What's your biggest takeaway from today?"

- "Can you think of another example?"

- "How could you apply this knowledge elsewhere?"

- "What surprised you about this?"

- "Let's discuss what worked well and why "

- "What does success look like to you?"

- "What questions do you still have?"

Classroom Management

"Let's all focus together "

"Please use your indoor voice "

"Raise your hand when you're ready to share "

"Let's keep our workspace clean "

"It's time to transition to the next activity "

"Please be respectful to everyone "

"Let's revisit our classroom norms "

"We're here to support each other "

"Silence can help us think deeply "

"Let's reset and try again "

Celebrating Success

"You nailed it!"

- *"Congratulations on your achievement!"*

- *"Let's give a round of applause "*

- *"You've exceeded expectations "*

- *"This deserves a celebration!"*

- *"Look how far you've come "*

- *"You're setting a great example "*

- *"I'm so proud of your growth "*

- *"Your hard work is paying off "*

- *"Let's share your success with others "*

Life Lessons

"Learning never stops "

"Be curious, not judgmental "

"Success is a journey, not a destination "

"Your character matters more than your grades "

"Integrity is doing the right thing when no one is watching "

"Kindness is never wasted "

"Your actions shape your future "

"You have the power to make a difference "

"Believe in yourself "

"Every day is a chance to grow "

Motivating Creativity and Innovation

"There's no wrong way to imagine "

"Think outside the box!"

"How can we make this even better?"

"Every idea starts somewhere "

"Let's experiment and see what happens "

"What's your unique solution?"

"How could we approach this differently?"

"Creativity takes courage—let's be brave!"

"Your imagination is your superpower "

"Don't be afraid to take creative risks "

Fostering Curiosity

"Why do you think this happens?"

- "What if we looked at this another way?"

- "What's a question you've always wanted to ask?"

- "How would you explain this to someone else?"

- "What can we discover together?"

- "Let's follow this question wherever it leads us "

- "Curiosity is the start of all learning "

- "What surprised you about this?"

- "Let's dig deeper into this topic "

- "What other questions does this make you think of?"

-

-

Subject-Specific Encouragement

"Math is all about problem-solving, not just numbers "

-

"Reading takes you to new worlds "

-

"Science helps us understand the world around us "

-

"History teaches us how the past shapes our future "

-

"Art is how we see the world in new ways "

-

"Writing is your chance to tell your story "

-

"Music is a language everyone can understand "

-

"Technology is a tool—you're the creator "

-

"Let's make this project your own "

-

"Every subject connects in some way "

-

-

Encouraging Growth Mindset

"Growth happens when we step out of our comfort zone "

"It's okay not to know everything yet "

"Effort creates ability "

"Failure is the first step toward success "

"Challenges make us stronger "

"Your brain is growing every time you learn "

"There's always a way forward "

"Every mistake is an opportunity to improve "

"Let's focus on progress, not perfection "

"You're capable of amazing things "

Social and Emotional Support

"How are you feeling today?"

- *"It's okay to ask for help "*

- *"You're never alone—we're a team "*

- *"Your feelings are valid "*

- *"Let's take a moment to breathe "*

- *"I'm here to listen if you need me "*

- *"Let's handle this together "*

- *"Everyone deserves kindness, including you "*

- *"You're stronger than you think "*

- *"Take it one step at a time "*

-

-

Instilling Responsibility and Accountability

"Take ownership of your learning "

"What could you do differently next time?"

"Let's talk about how to make this right "

"Being responsible means thinking about others too "

"Your choices shape your outcomes "

"Let's set a goal and stick to it "

"Responsibility is a skill—practice makes perfect "

"What steps will you take to improve?"

"Own your success, and learn from setbacks "

"Accountability builds trust "

Celebrating Individuality

"Your uniqueness is your strength "

"The world needs your perspective "

"Everyone has something valuable to contribute "

"Your voice matters "

"Let's embrace what makes you different "

"Celebrate your achievements, big or small "

"How can you share your talents today?"

"Diversity is what makes our class strong "

"Be proud of who you are "

"Your individuality inspires others "

Building Teamwork and Collaboration

"We're stronger together "

"What can we achieve as a team?"

"Teamwork takes practice—let's try again "

"How can you help your classmate succeed?"

"Collaboration makes our ideas better "

"Let's brainstorm together "

"Great teams listen to everyone's input "

"Your contribution matters to the group "

"What did you learn from working with others?"

"Teamwork is about sharing strengths "

Promoting a Positive Mindset

"Every day is a fresh start "

"Let's focus on the positives "

"What's something good that happened today?"

"A smile can brighten someone's day "

"Let's find the silver lining "

"You have the power to change your mood "

"Positivity creates possibility "

"Let's tackle this challenge with optimism "

"Your mindset shapes your outcomes "

"Celebrate the little victories "

Encouraging Exploration and Curiosity

"What if we tried looking at this another way?"

"Questions are the beginning of discovery "

"Let's dig deeper into that idea "

"What makes you curious today?"

"Every question leads to a new adventure "

"There's always more to learn "

"How can we explore this further?"

"Let's investigate and find out!"

"Curiosity keeps the world exciting "

"Never stop asking 'Why?'"

Fostering Respect and Inclusivity

"Treat others the way you want to be treated "

- "How can we make everyone feel included?"

- "Respect is the foundation of great relationships "

- "Let's listen to understand, not just reply "

- "Appreciate others' perspectives "

- "Kindness makes a difference "

- "What did you learn from someone different from you?"

- "Our classroom is a safe space for all "

- "Diversity enriches our experience "

- "Respect everyone's journey "

Motivating Problem-Solving and Critical Thinking

"What are the different ways we can approach this?"

- "Mistakes are clues to the solution "

- "How would you explain this to someone else?"

- "Can you think of a real-world example?"

- "What's another way to solve this?"

- "Let's break it into smaller steps "

- "What's the first thing you notice?"

- "How does this connect to what we already know?"

- "Great problem solvers think creatively "

- "Why do you think that solution works?"

-

-

Celebrating Growth and Effort

"Look at how much you've improved!"

"You should be so proud of your progress "

"Every small step counts towards big success "

"Your hard work is paying off!"

"It's exciting to see your growth "

"The effort you put in is inspiring "

"Learning is a marathon, not a sprint "

"Keep going—your persistence will pay off "

"You've come so far already!"

"Celebrate every little victory "

Building Student Ownership of Learning

"What's your plan to tackle this?"

- "How will you know when you've mastered this?"

- "What's one thing you can do differently next time?"

- "Tell me about your learning process today "

- "How would you rate your effort and why?"

- "What do you think your next step should be?"

- "Who or what could help you solve this?"

- "What's a goal you can set for yourself here?"

- "How does this topic relate to your interests?"

- "Why is this important to you?"

-

-

Encouraging Creativity and Innovation

"What's a completely unique way to approach this?"

- *"Imagine if there were no limits—what would you do?"*

- *"What story could you tell through this work?"*

- *"There's no wrong answer here—let's brainstorm!"*

- *"Think outside the box—what's another possibility?"*

- *"How would you design this if you were in charge?"*

- *"What's a bold idea you could try?"*

- *"What inspires you when working on projects like this?"*

- *"You have the freedom to think big—what will you create?"*

- *"Your imagination is your only limit!"*

-

-

-

Promoting Collaboration and Teamwork

"How can you support each other in this activity?"

- "What are the strengths each of you brings to this group?"

- "Let's make sure everyone's voice is heard "

- "How can you divide this task fairly?"

- "What can we accomplish together that we couldn't do alone?"

- "What did you learn from your teammate today?"

- "Is there a way to combine your ideas?"

- "How can you resolve this conflict respectfully?"

- "Great teamwork makes big dreams work!"

- "What role would you like to take in this project?"

Encouraging Lifelong Learning

"What's something new you've learned outside of school lately?"

- "Let's keep growing together!"

- "Every expert was once a beginner "

- "Where do you see this knowledge helping you in the future?"

- "How can you apply what you learned today in real life?"

- "Curiosity is your superpower—keep asking questions!"

- "What would you like to learn more about?"

- "Learning doesn't stop when the bell rings."

- "Knowledge is your toolkit—add to it every day."

- "What inspires you to keep exploring?"

-

-

Fostering Confidence and Encouraging Risk-Taking

"You can do this; I believe in you."

- *"Mistakes are part of learning."*

- *"It's okay to try and fail; it's a step toward success."*

- *"Take your time, and don't rush."*

- *"What's the worst that can happen if you try?"*

- *"Let's see how we can improve this next time."*

- *"You're on the right track!"*

- *"I'm proud of how hard you're working."*

- *"Think of this as an opportunity to grow."*

- *"Your effort is just as important as a result"*

Inspiring Critical Thinking

"Why do you think that is the case?"

- *"Can you back up that idea with evidence?"*

- *"What's another way you could approach this problem?"*

- *"What would happen if we did it differently?"*

- *"How can you support that argument?"*

- *"What's the bigger picture here?"*

- *"Let's look at this from another perspective "*

- *"Can you identify any patterns here?"*

- *"What other solutions can we brainstorm?"*

- *"Why is this important in the real world?"*

Motivating Growth and Persistence

"You're improving every day."

"Keep going; you're getting closer to the answer!"

"Great job! Now, let's see if we can go even further."

"Every small step you take is progress."

"What did you learn from that mistake?"

"Let's set a new goal together."

"Persistence is the key to success."

"Believe in your potential and push your limits."

"Your effort today will pay off tomorrow."

"Let's try one more time and improve."

Encouraging Critical Thinking and Inquiry

"What do you think the answer might be?"

- "Can you explain how you arrived at that conclusion?"

- "What evidence do you have to support your idea?"

- "How does this relate to what we learned before?"

- "What are some other possible solutions?"

- "Why do you think this is important?"

- "Can you compare this idea with another one?"

- "What would happen if you approached this differently?"

- "Let's challenge this thought—what if it's false?"

- "Why is this perspective valuable?"

-

-

Fostering Motivation and Engagement

"I believe you can do this!"

"Your effort today shows your growth!"

"Great job, keep up the hard work!"

"Your creativity is inspiring!"

"You're getting better each day!"

"Don't give up, I know you're capable!"

"This challenge is just another opportunity to grow!"

"Mistakes are proof that you're learning."

"You've come so far; be proud of yourself!"

"You're not just learning the content; you're learning how to think!"

"Your perseverance will pay off."

"Let's find a way to make this easier for you."

"This is a great start; let's build on that."

"What's one thing you could try differently next time?"

"I appreciate your effort; keep pushing forward!"

"How can we make this even better?"

"You've got this; I'm here to help if you need it!"

"It's okay to ask questions—that's how we learn."

"Let's take a break and come back with fresh eyes."

"Every day is a new opportunity to grow!"

"You've made a lot of progress; keep it up!"

"Let's try a different approach."

"I believe in your ability to succeed."

"Everyone learns at their own pace."

How can I help you understand this better?"

Mistakes are proof that you're trying."

"It's okay to take your time with this."

You're doing great; keep going!"

"Learning is a journey, not a race."

"What's your next goal? Let's work towards it."

"Your effort today will lead to progress tomorrow."

"I can see you're putting in much hard work."

"Think about it for a moment before answering."

"We're all learning together."

- *"Every day is a chance to improve."*

- *"Let's try to solve this problem step by step."*

- *"It's okay to feel challenged—growth happens here."*

- *"I love the way you're thinking."*

- *"Learning is not about being perfect; it's about progress."*

- *"You have a bright mind; let's explore it further."*

"Mistakes are a part of the learning process."

"Let's work together to figure this out."

"You are capable of more than you think."

"It's important to listen to understand, not just to respond."

"Can you explain your reasoning behind that?"

"What other approaches could we try?"

"Every question you ask helps us all learn."

"I appreciate how you supported your classmate."

"Learning is not a race; it's a journey."

"Believe in your ability to overcome challenges."

"Let's celebrate the progress you've made today."

"What's the first step we should take here?"

"That's an interesting perspective; tell me more."

"You did a great job collaborating with your team."

- *"Remember, every expert was once a beginner."*

- *"How can we approach this problem differently?"*

- *"I appreciate your effort and determination."*

- *"Learning is about growth, not perfection."*

- *"Take your time; there's no rush to understand this."*

- *"Your creativity adds so much to this discussion."*

-

"Your unique perspective is a gift to this group."

"It's okay not to get it right the first time."

"What connections can you make between these ideas?"

"Mistakes are proof that you're learning something new."

"Can you teach this concept to a classmate?"

"Your input makes our discussions richer."

"Let's look at this challenge from another angle."

"How do you think you've improved this week?"

"What's one thing you're proud of today?"

"Your perseverance inspires everyone around you."

"How can you apply this in your daily life?"

"Great teamwork, everyone!"

"What steps can you take to overcome this hurdle?"

"Let's celebrate small wins today."

- *"I believe in your ability to succeed."*

- *"What's one thing you'd like to improve tomorrow?"*

- *"Can you think of another way to approach this problem?"*

- *"Let's take a moment to reflect on what we've learned."*

- *"You are capable of amazing growth."*

- *"What part of this was the most challenging for you?"*

-

Keep up the good work.

I believe in you

- *You are capable of great things*

- *Mistakes are opportunities to learn*

- *You can do hard things*

- *Let's try a different approach*

- *Your effort is paying off*

- *I appreciate your hard work*

- *I'm proud of you*

- *What are your thoughts on this?*

- *It's okay to ask for help*

- *Let's break it down step by step*

- *Practice makes progress*

- *Learning is a journey, not a race*

- Let's collaborate on this

- What are you curious about today?

- Use your resources wisely

- Let's explore that idea further

- How can we approach this challenge?

- Your perseverance is inspiring

- In what ways can you improve?

- Trust in your abilities

- Stay positive and keep going

- It's okay to make mistakes

- What can we learn from this experience?

- Your growth is significant to me

Your creativity shines through

Embrace the process of learning

Challenge yourself to reach new heights

Let's celebrate your progress

You have a unique perspective to offer

Remember, progress over perfection

Take a moment to reflect on your work

Your determination is commendable

What do you need to succeed?

Find joy in the learning journey.

Your resilience is impressive

Let's find a way to make this fun

You make a difference in this classroom

Your effort is making a difference

- *What questions do you have for me?*

- *Stay focused on your goals*

- *Your passion for learning is evident*

- *Believe in yourself as I believe in you*

- *Your contributions are valued*

- *How can we apply what you've learned?*

- *Let's foster a culture of kindness*

- *Always strive to improve*

- *You have the power to make a positive impact*

- *Your uniqueness is your strength*

- *Let's learn from each other*

- *Your determination is inspiring others*

Embrace challenges as opportunities to grow

- *Your enthusiasm is contagious*

- *Trust the process of learning*

- *What can you teach me today?*

- *Keep pushing yourself to do your best*

- *Take risks and learn from them*

- *Your dedication is admirable*

- *Let's create a supportive learning environment*

-

Your hard work is paying off.

In what ways can you build on your strengths?

- *Your insights are valuabl.e*

- *What are you most proud of today?*

- *Stay curious and keep exploring.*

- *Your commitment to learning is evident*

- *Let's strive for progress, not perfection*

- *Your diligence is appreciated*

- *How can we overcome this challenge together?*

- *Stay open to new ideas and perspectives*

- *You have a voice that deserves to be heard*

- *Let's learn from our mistakes and move forward*

- *Your growth mindset is impressive*

- *Your determination is setting a great example*

- *Take pride in your accomplishments*

- *Your positive attitude is contagious*

- *Keep challenging yourself to reach new heights*

- *Let's approach this with a growth mindset*

- *Your resilience is a strength*

- *Your commitment to learning is inspiring*

You have the potential to achieve great things

Embrace the learning process with an open mind

- *Let's work together to find a solution*

- *Your willingness to learn is commendable*

- *Make mistakes, learn, and grow*

- *Your effort is making a difference*

- *Let's believe in our ability to succeed*

- *Keep pushing yourself to exceed your limits*

- *Your creativity adds value to our discussions*

- *Your input is valuable to our learning journey*

- *Let's learn from our experiences, both good and bad*

- *Your hard work does not go unnoticed*

- *Let's embrace challenges as opportunities for growth*

- *Your commitment to learning is inspiring*

- *Your determination to succeed is commendable*

- *Let's approach this task with a positive mindset*

- *Your willingness to try new things makes a difference*

- *Keep aiming for progress, not perfection*

- *Your resilience in the face of challenges is admirable*

- *Let's celebrate all the ways you have grown and succeeded*

-

-

Your dedication to learning is commendable.

Let's learn from each other's perspectives.

- *Your ability to adapt to new challenges is impressive*

- *Keep pushing yourself out of your comfort zone*

- *Your willingness to take initiative is valued*

- *Let's approach this problem with a growth mindset*

- *Your enthusiasm for learning is infectious*

- *Don't be afraid to make mistakes and learn from them*

- *Your commitment to self-improvement is inspiring*

- *Let's encourage a culture of continuous learning*

- *Your resilience in the face of adversity is remarkable*

- *Stay focused on your goals, and you will succeed*

- *Your attention to detail is appreciated*

- *Let's explore new ways to approach this topic*

- *Your ability to think critically is a valuable skill*

- *Keep challenging yourself to think outside the box*

- *Your honesty in self-assessment is commendable*

- *Let's strive for excellence in everything we do*

- *Your positive attitude towards challenges is refreshing*

- *Embrace the power of yet – you may not know something yet, but you will*

- Your ability to think creatively sets you apart

- Let's find joy in learning, not just the result

- Your kindness towards others makes a difference

- Your commitment to growth and development is admirable

- Keep shining with your unique talents and abilities

- Let's discover the beauty of learning from our mistakes

- Your openness to feedback is a sign of maturity

- Your inquisitive nature is a key to unlocking knowledge

- Embrace the uncertainty of learning – it's where growth happens

Your resilience in the face of failure is a testament to your character

- *Your willingness to help others shows authentic leadership*

- *Keep embracing challenges as opportunities for growth*

- *Let's cultivate a sense of curiosity and wonder in our learning*

- *Your ability to ask thoughtful questions is a sign of intelligence*

- *Your determination to overcome obstacles is inspiring*

- *Your willingness to support your classmates is heartwarming*

- *Let's foster a community of respect and understanding*

- *Your ability to listen attentively is a valuable skill*

- *Your positive impact on others is immeasurable*

- *Keep striving for progress, even in small steps*

Your compassion towards others is commendable.

Let's approach each day as a new opportunity to learn and grow

- *Your dedication to self-improvement is evident*

- *Your patience in the learning process is admirable*

- *Your commitment to excellence sets a high standard for us all*

- *Let's embrace the diversity of perspectives in our learning environment*

- *Your willingness to share your knowledge is appreciated*

- *Your leadership qualities shine through in your actions*

- *Keep curious about the world around you – it's where learning begins*

- *Your determination to succeed is unwavering.*

2

About the Author

Dheeraj Mehrotra, a white and a yellow belt in SIX SIGMA, a Certified NLP Business Diploma holder, is an Educational Innovator, Author, with expertise in Six Sigma In Education, Academic Audits, Neuro-Linguistic Programming (NLP), Total Quality Management In Education, an Experiential Educator, a CBSE Resource towards School Assessment (SQAA), CCE, JIT, Five S, and KAIZEN. He has authored over 100 books on computer science, AI, digital body language, NLP, quality circles, school management, classroom effectiveness, and safety and security.

A former Principal at De Indian Public School, New Delhi, (INDIA), NPS International School, Guwahati, Kunwar's Global School, Lucknow and an Education Officer at GEMS, Gurgaon, with ample teaching experience of over Three Decades, he is a certified Trainer for Quality Circles/ TQM in Education and QCI Standards for School Accreditation/ School Audits and Management. He has also been honoured with the President of India's National Teacher Award in 2006 and the Best Science Teacher State Award (By the Ministry of Science and Technology, State of UP), among others. He has published over 100 books and developed 150 FREE EDUCATIONAL MOBILE Apps for the Google Play Store exclusively for Teachers, Students, and Parents.

This work has been recognised by the LIMCA BOOK OF RECORDS and INDIA BOOK OF RECORDS as the only Indian to draw that feast. As a premium UDEMY Instructor, he has developed over 500 courses and caters to over 8 Lakh students from 180 countries. As a founder and president of the IoT Society of India, he also promotes Technology Globally.

Dr Mehrotra is presently engaged as a REGIONAL HEAD of the GEMS EDUCATION India Region.

3
Books By The Same Author

www.authordheerajmehrotra.com

www.ingramcontent.com/pod-product-compliance
Lightning Source LLC
Chambersburg PA
CBHW040122150726
48005CB00015B/2334